TITHE

TAPPING THE NETWORK OF HEAVEN

NEIL KENNEDY

Introduction

I did not grow up in the Church, so when I converted to Christ, I had a lot to learn. Tithing was something that I knew nothing about. I found out that Tithing was expected without question; however, it was also without teaching.

I was left with assumptions.

The first assumption was that it was some sort of church tax system. I was used to paying Federal, State, Social Security, and local taxes, so now I am paying a church tax. Just put it on my tab!

My second assumption was that it was part of the religious Law based on the Old Testament. Although I grasped that the New Testament accepted me by grace, I assumed I was still expected to live up to the Law of Tithing.

Again, I couldn't find teaching on the subject. I never once heard my pastor teach on it. He was reluctant, and many were that day, to approach the subject. They relegated the topic of giving to be taught by TV evangelists, some teaching for self-gain. Truthfully, several ministers teaching on television opened my eyes to see a lot of Scriptures on the subject.

Many of them helped me discover many truths regarding Biblical Economics. The second book I wrote was **God's Currency: The Entrepreneurial Drive.** I want you to have a copy [*https://bit.ly/godscurrency*], or if you would like, you can get a hard copy at FivestarMan.com/books.

I now have close to 40 years of teaching ministry. I have started my ministry with nothing and have had to believe God for everything. Starting two churches, funding them, beginning a travel ministry of consulting, and founding FivestarMan.com have required me to learn much about Biblical Economics.

I preached a message entitled, **Redeemed to Profit** at a great church in the Atlanta area. The Lead Pastor told me that his tithes and offerings grew exponentially afterward. Recently, I preached that message at Evangel World Harvest, led by Dr. Bob Rogers, who complimented, "Neil, I've never heard a better message on Tithing."

Because of that, I decided to share the foundations of Tithing with you in this book. You will discover some truths that completely change your financial outlook, especially in chapter six, **The Window: Portal to the Unseen Realm**. You need the foundation of the first five chapters before you get there.

Let me give you an appetizer for it.

I am sitting in a room, a box surrounded by walls. A window is over my left shoulder. I cannot see beyond the walls, but I can see through the window outside. The window allows me to be in one space and see another place. The open window allows me access to a portal outside of my box.

Similarly, when God promises to "open the windows of heaven, " he says he wants to give you access out of your box of time and see into the unseen realm.

He says that the Tithe is the protocol to tap the network of Heaven.

Or consider your phone. It really is a window. The phone is a tablet of glass that allows you to tap into a global network of knowledge, commerce, communication, etc.

To access the global network, you must use the internet protocol.

The Tithe is the protocol to tap into the network of Heaven.

One day, I asked the LORD what I could do to reach more men with the message of FivestarMan.com. His Spirit prompted me to read Habakkuk 2:2:

> *"Write my answer **plainly on tablets,**
> so that a runner can carry the correct message to others.*
> *This vision is for a future time.*
> *It describes the end, and it will be fulfilled.*
> *If it seems slow, wait patiently,*
> *for it will surely take place.*
> *It will not be delayed."*

For the first time, I saw the word ***tablets*** in a very different light. I realized that we can now reach every man who carries a phone with the message of FivestarMan.com. This revelation changed our strategies when we created the FivestarMan 45-Day Challenge, which reaches thousands of men. It inspires men through the Challenge and empowers them to tell their friends, coworkers, and family members about the positive changes the challenge has had on their lives.

I am excited about this book because I know hundreds of men will start Tithing in worship, experience an open portal to the unseen realm, and tap into Heaven's network. These men will be propelled out of poverty and discover the true meaning of purposed prosperity—they will have the means to fulfill their meaning.

I expect you to be one of them.

The Genesis of Giving

Genesis 1:29
Then God said, "I give you every seed-bearing plant on the face of the whole earth and every tree that has fruit with seed in it. They will be yours for food."

The Genesis of Giving Begins with God

God is a giver by nature. The very first gift He bestowed upon humanity was the gift of seed-bearing plants. This was no ordinary gift—it was extraordinary. With it, God equipped mankind to meet every conceivable need, fulfilling not only immediate sustenance but ensuring a perpetual cycle of provision through the seed.

2 Corinthians 9:10
"Now he who supplies seed to the sower and bread for food will also supply and increase

your store of seed and will enlarge the harvest of your righteousness."

If you desire to reflect God's nature, you will become a giver. Giving originates with God, the Source of all provision. Our giving is not self-initiated; it is a response to the abundant generosity He first demonstrated.

From Abundance to Curse: The Impact of Disobedience

Adam and Eve began in abundance, living in the Garden of Eden—a divine storehouse of provision. Every seed had potential, every river enriched the soil, and every tree yielded beauty and nourishment.

One tree, however, was sacred. God's explicit instruction was to leave the tree of the knowledge of good and evil untouched. Not all knowledge is good, and God wanted man to be protected from the bad knowledge.

Even though man had access to it doesn't mean that it would be beneficial to him to have it.

Genesis 2:15-17

"The Lord God took the man and put him in the Garden of Eden to work it and take care of it. And the Lord God commanded the man, 'You are free to eat from any tree in the garden; but you must not eat from the tree of the knowledge of good and evil, for when you eat from it you will certainly die.'"

This single act of disobedience was Adam's stewardship test. Yet, when Adam violated God's command, he embezzled what belonged to the Creator. The consequence was the curse of poverty and struggle. Adam and Eve were expelled from the Garden, and their descendants, including Cain and Abel, were born into hardship.

Marriage: Agreement and Authority

It wasn't meant to be this way.

God sees that Adam is alone in his work and requires a perfect companion to walk and work in agreement with him—a helper.

At this moment, a unique exercise happens. God parades the animals to walk in front of Adam.

Adam is responsible for naming the animals because God has given him dominion over them. It also distinguishes Adam from all creatures.

Although humans were created with similarities, there is a vast chasm between animals and humans. Humans were made after the image of God and reflected His likeness. Seeing this distinction firsthand was essential to Adam.

By displaying this, God is telling Adam, "You are not to be like the animals; you are to be like Me."

God then puts Adam to sleep and extracts a bone. Out of the bone, God makes a suitable Helper, named woman ('iššâ). She is beautiful and has a perfect complementary design to walk equally beside her husband. Together, they form a bond of agreement—marriage. With marriage, Adam and Eve are the superiors of the earth, capable of anything. If two agree on earth, God will agree in heaven.

Matthew 18:19
Again, truly I tell you that if two of you on earth agree about anything they ask for, it will be done for them by my Father in heaven. For

where two or three gather in my name, there am I with them.

Agreement within marriage is a powerful force.

However, agreement requires clear communication and shared purpose. Husbands, your responsibility is to hear from God and lead your wife in faith. Wives must hear your vision to walk in alignment.

Amos 3:3
"Can two walk together, except they be agreed?"

Marriage is not a competition; it is a covenant of completion. When a husband and wife stand united, their work is blessed, their strength is multiplied, and their bond is unbreakable.

**Marriage is designed for completion,
not for competition.**

Let me take a moment and speak to the above statement.

Husbands, you have a responsibility to hear from God. Then, after you have heard from Him, you must turn to your wife and give her faith to follow you.

How do two walk together unless you agree on the destination?

This foundation in marriage will become critical in our future discussion of the Tithe.

Amos 3:3

Can two walk together, except they are agreed?

Ecclesiastes 4:9-12

Two are better than one, because they have a good return for their labor: [10]If either of them falls down, one can help the other up.
But pity anyone who falls and has no one to help them up. [11]Also, if two lie down together, they will keep warm. But how can one keep warm alone? [12]Though one may be overpowered, two can defend themselves. A cord of three strands is not quickly broken.

Five Keys to Walking in Agreement According to Ecclesiastes 4:9-12

1. **Mutual Benefit**

   Two get a better return for their work. Their work was blessed as long as Adam and Eve walked in accord.

2. **Shared Warmth**

   If two people lie down together, they will keep warm. Lying together creates a warm connection and intimacy. I strongly recommend that you stay in the same bed at night. When King David was old and chilled, Abishag became his concubine to keep him warm.

3. **Combined Strength**

   "And though a man might prevail against one alone, two will withstand him—a threefold cord is not quickly broken." We have opponents. We must have a marriage that stands together against those who oppose us.

4. **Unity in Purpose**

   Walking in agreement requires shared goals and a unified front. If either party in the relationship is unaware of the purpose, they will not agree.

5. **Open Communication**
    Honest and open communication is essential for resolving conflicts and maintaining unity. It is giving faith to follow. Your wife must hear from you to believe and trust where you're going. Faith comes by hearing, and hearing comes by the Word. Likewise, her confidence in direction will come from hearing from you.

However, an enemy of marriage, the Deceiver, desires to bring a wedge between the husband and wife. He will use a variety of schemes that we should not be ignorant of.

The subtle skill of deception is evident in the snake's approach to Eve. First, the snake usurped the husband's authority to approach Eve. Adam served the LORD under the protocol of authority, which is designed to protect, provide, promote, and empower those within it.

Ephesians 5:21-27
Submit to one another out of reverence for Christ. Wives, submit yourselves to your husbands as you do to the Lord. For the husband is the head of the wife as Christ is

the head of the church, his body, of which he is the Savior. Now that the church submits to Christ, wives should also submit to their husbands in everything.

Husbands love your wives, just as Christ loved the church and gave himself up for her to make her holy, cleansing her by the washing with water through the word, and to present her to himself as a radiant church, without stain or wrinkle or any other blemish, but holy and blameless.

Paul reveals a clear protocol of authority that is designed to protect us from deceptive forces:

- **Christ is submitted to the Father.**
  John 8:28: *"When you have lifted up the Son of Man, then you will know that I am he and that I do nothing on my own but speak just what the Father has taught me."* It is not demeaning for Christ, who is equal to the Father, to serve in submission to the Father.
- **Men are submitted to Christ.**
  Verse 21, *"Submit to one another out of reverence for Christ."* Also, James 4:7: *"Submit*

yourselves therefore to God. Resist the devil, and he will flee from you." It is not demeaning for a man to be submitted to God through Christ.

- **Wives are submitted to their husbands.** Verse 22, *"Submit yourselves to your husbands as you do to the Lord."* It is not demeaning for wives to be submitted to their husbands.
- **Children are submitted to their parents.** Ephesians 6:3: *"This is the first commandment with a promise: If you honor your father and mother, 'Things will go well for you, and you will have a long life on the earth.'"* It is not demeaning for children to be submitted to their parents.

The Protocol protects, provides, promotes, and empowers through the line of authority. It begins with the Word of the Father, revealed in Christ, who is the Word that became flesh, spoken, and received by men and women to raise godly offspring.

The husband is directed to love their wives as Christ loves the Church and uses the Word to protect them from deception.

This warning is appropriate because Adam failed to protect his wife from the snake. Adam was given dominion over everything that crept on the ground. All Adam had to do was put his foot down. Unfortunately, he allowed the snake to question God's Word and bring doubt to her identity.

Men, there will be times when you must 'put your foot down' to protect your wife, your home, and your work.

The Deceiver's Scheme

The serpent's approach to Eve was deliberate, undermining the protocol of authority God had established.

Genesis 3:1
"Did God really say, 'You must not eat from any tree in the garden'?"

The serpent's strategy was deception, introducing doubt and twisting God's Word. Eve's response revealed misunderstanding: "You must not touch it," she added—an addition not commanded by God. The serpent exploited this misstep, persuading her to disobey.

Adam failed to protect his wife. As the one given dominion over creation, Adam should have silenced the serpent. His abdication of responsibility opened the door to sin.

Sin opened the door to poverty, destruction, and death.

They were expelled from the Garden. Adam was terminated from his job. His property was repossessed. An angelic guard was assigned to protect the Trees from Adam's mismanagement. He hid in shame and lost the respect of his wife. His sons were born into poverty.
His work became labor.

Adam could no longer be trusted with God's gift of seed. He became nomadic, wandering the Earth looking for a purpose and laboring against thorns and thistles.

Eve was assigned pain during childbirth. Adam was assigned pain in work.

This is the environment that Cain and Abel are born into: poverty, subsistence living, or, as we say, "living pay-check to pay-check."

Something had to change.

Change will only happen when the pain of staying the same is greater than the pain of doing something different.

> *Hebrews 11:4*
> *"By faith, Abel brought God a better offering than Cain did. By faith, he was commended as righteous when God spoke well of his offerings. And by faith, Abel still speaks, even though he is dead."*

Abel stands as the first recorded man of faith. Think about being the first man ever recorded to have faith.

Consider this: Abel, amidst the trials of life, inherently recognized that God was worthy of worship. His response was to offer the firstborn of his flock—an act of gratitude and reverence. We must delve into what drove him to this expression to grasp the significance of Abel's faith.

The First Offerings: A Distinction of Heart

Genesis 4:2-5

"Now Abel kept flocks, and Cain worked the soil. In the course of time, Cain brought some of the fruits of the soil as an offering to the Lord. And Abel also brought an offering—fat portions from some of the firstborn of his flock. The Lord looked with favor on Abel and his offering, but on Cain and his offering, he did not look with favor. So Cain was very angry, and his face was downcast."

The first recorded offerings to God were given by two brothers, Cain and Abel. Yet, one offering pleased God, while the other did not. Why? The answer lies in the quality and heart behind the gifts.

Cain presented "some of the fruits," while Abel gave the "fat portions of the firstborn."

Cain's offering was casual; Abel's was intentional. The distinction was not the type of offering—plants versus livestock—but the motivation and apportionment. Abel brought the first and best, while Cain merely brought some.

Throughout Scripture, God honors the first—the Tithe.

This principle reflects faith and trust in God as the ultimate provider. Abel's offering revealed a heart of faith, while Cain's exposed indifference.

Cain gave a tip; Abel gave the Tithe.

Tithe

Faith In Action: Abel's Legacy

Abel stands as a towering figure in the story of humanity—not for his strength, wealth, or position, but for his faith.

Remember, Abel was born into desperate poverty due to his father's embezzlement. He deeply desired to turn his labor into favor.

But how could he break through the barrier of mediocrity and restore wealth to his life and family?

Abel was the first man to express faith in God through giving. His offering was more than a ritual; it was an act of worship, trust, and reverence. His legacy teaches us the profound faith aspect of tithing and what it means to give to God by faith, not sight.

The Faith of Abel: Tithing as Worship

Hebrews 11:4

"By faith Abel brought God a better offering than Cain did. By faith he was commended as righteous when God spoke well of his offerings. And by faith Abel still speaks, even though he is dead."

Abel's act of giving was rooted in faith. While his brother Cain presented some of his produce, Abel gave the first and best portions of the firstborn of his flock. His offering was not merely a portion of his income but the most valuable part—the firstborn. This was his Tithe.

Abel's faith demonstrated three essential truths about Tithing:

1. **Tithing as an Act of Worship**
   Abel's gift wasn't just about the material value of what he gave. It was about honoring God as the Source of all he had. By giving the first and best, Abel acknowledged God's sovereignty and demonstrated his dependence on Him.

2. **Faith Over Fear**
    Abel didn't hold back, wondering if more
    flocks would come. He gave in faith, trusting
    that the God who provided the firstborn
    would continue to provide.
3. **A Response to God's Character**
    Abel's offering revealed his understanding of
    who God is—a gracious provider who is
    worthy of the best.

Giving by Faith, Not by Sight

2 Corinthians 5:7
"For we live by faith, not by sight."

You will never give your best if you do not believe
in the best of God's character.

To give by faith means to trust in God's provision
rather than relying on what you see or have at
the moment.

Abel's story illustrates this beautifully. He gave
his firstborn lambs when he could not yet see
how his flock would multiply. By offering the best
before ensuring his own future security, Abel
declared his confidence in God's faithfulness.

This principle remains true today. Giving the first 10%—the tithe—requires faith, especially when resources seem limited. It demands trust in the promise that God will meet your needs and bless your obedience.

Approaching God with Faith

Hebrews 11:6
"And without faith it is impossible to please God, because anyone who comes to him must believe that he exists and that he rewards those who earnestly seek him."

Abel approached God with faith, believing that He is both real and responsive. Faithful giving is an expression of seeking God earnestly, trusting Him to be the Rewarder of those who put Him first.

When we tithe by faith, we declare:

- **God is my Provider.**
  Tithing affirms that your trust is not in your job, your business, or your abilities, but in God's unlimited resources.

- **God is faithful to His Word.**
  The tithe is a test of trust. When we obey, we align ourselves with His promises to provide and bless.
- **God is worthy of my best.**
  Giving by faith means offering the first and best portion—not what's left over—because God deserves our best.

Practical Steps to Give in Faith

Faith in action requires intentionality. Here are practical steps to help you give in faith, following Abel's example.

Prioritize the Tithe

Set aside the first 10% of your income for God before you allocate resources to anything else. This intentional act demonstrates trust and honors Him as your Provider.

Pray Over Your Giving

Have confidence that what you are doing is an act of worship. You're not paying a bill. You are expressing your faith. Before you tithe, take a moment to pray. Acknowledge God as the source of your provision and express your trust in His faithfulness.

Give Joyfully

2 Corinthians 9:7 reminds us, "God loves a cheerful giver." Faith-filled giving is not done grudgingly or out of obligation but with joy, knowing that God delights in your trust.

Align with God's Promises

Anchor your giving in Scripture. Meditate on verses like Malachi 3:10, which promises that God will "open the windows of heaven and pour out blessings" for those who tithe. Let His Word fuel your faith.

Trust Beyond Immediate Results

Faithful giving doesn't always yield instant results, but trust that God's timing is perfect. Continue to sow faithfully, believing in His ability to reward and provide abundantly.

Faith as a Tangible Substance

Hebrews 11:1-2 (NKJV)

"Now faith is the substance of things hoped for,

the evidence of things not seen. For by it the elders obtained a good testimony."

Faith is often perceived as an abstract, intangible concept—a mere belief or mental assent to something we cannot physically touch. However, Hebrews 11:1 challenges this misconception by describing faith as something very real, very tangible, and with a substance that is as concrete as any material thing.

The writer of Hebrews gives us a powerful understanding of faith that moves beyond mere thinking or imagining—it's a force that has the power to shape reality.

1. Faith as the Substance of Things Hoped For

The first phrase in Hebrews 11:1 says, *"faith is the substance of things hoped for."*

The word "substance" here comes from the Greek word **hupostasis**, which means "standing under" or "foundation."

It is the same concept as the Protocol of Authority that we spoke of earlier. It refers to the essence, reality, or the very structure that underpins something. In essence, faith is the foundation upon which our hope rests.

Faith is not a fleeting feeling or wishful thinking. It is the bedrock of our expectations and the assurance that what we hope for will come to pass. Just as a building needs a strong foundation to stand firm, our hopes and dreams—those things we are believing for—are anchored in the solid substance of faith. Faith gives our hopes substance; it makes them real and tangible in the spiritual realm.

To illustrate this, imagine a blueprint for a building. The blueprint is a picture of something that has not yet been built, but faith acts as the material that will bring that blueprint into physical reality. In the same way, the desires and promises we have are not mere fantasies—they have weight and structure when viewed through the lens of faith. Faith is the "material" that shapes them.

2. Faith as the Evidence of Things Not Seen

The next part of Hebrews 11:1 tells us that faith is "the evidence of things not seen." The word "evidence" here comes from the Greek word *elegchos*, which refers to proof, conviction, or a demonstration of something that is real. In legal terms, evidence is used to support the truth of a claim. Similarly, faith is the evidence that supports the truth of God's promises, even though we may not yet see them with our natural eyes.

Faith makes the unseen visible in the spiritual realm, even when our natural senses perceive no tangible proof. It is like a legal document that proves ownership or a receipt that guarantees a purchase. In the unseen realm, faith operates as the proof that what God has promised will come to fruition.

This is where many people get confused: they think that faith is something mystical or disconnected from reality. But faith is deeply grounded in the truth of God's Word. When we believe God for something—whether it's healing, provision, peace, or a breakthrough—we may not immediately see it, but our faith is the evidence that God's promises are sure and will come to pass. Just as a building is real and tangible when the blueprint is followed, our hopes become tangible when they are rooted in faith.

3. Faith is Not a Mystical Idea; It is a Tangible Force

While faith may be invisible to the naked eye, it is not mystical or ethereal. Faith is a force that has substance, impact, and power. It is a real, tangible thing in the spiritual realm that can shape the physical world. To understand this, we need to look at the lives of those who have lived by faith, as Hebrews 11:2 tells us, "For by it the elders obtained a good testimony." These "elders" or heroes of the faith demonstrated that faith is something far more than mere belief; it is something that produces results.

Consider the examples given in Hebrews 11—the lives of Abel, Noah, Abraham, Sarah, Moses, and others. These men and women did not merely hope in the abstract. Their faith produced tangible results. Abel's offering was accepted by God because it was offered in faith (Hebrews

11:4). Noah built an ark because he believed God's warning about an unseen flood (Hebrews 11:7). Abraham left his homeland to pursue a promise of descendants and land that he could not yet see (Hebrews 11:8-10). These are not acts of blind faith or mystical experiences; they are grounded in the concrete substance of trust in God's Word.

In the same way, when we put our faith in God's promises, we are engaging with a tangible, powerful force. Faith is not just a vague or abstract concept; it is the real, spiritual substance that brings the unseen into the seen. It enables us to receive the promises of God, even if those promises are not yet visible to the human eye.

4. The Practical Application: Faith in Action

So, what does this mean for us in a practical sense? If faith is a tangible substance and evidence, then it requires action. Faith is not passive. It demands that we act in accordance with what we believe, even when we do not yet see the fulfillment of our hopes.

Believe God's Promises

The first step is to believe that God's promises are real and that they are for you. Read the Scriptures, and take God's promises to heart. Faith comes by hearing the Word of God (Romans 10:17), so fill your mind with what God has said about you and your situation.

Act on Your Faith

Faith without action is dead (James 2:17). Just as Noah built the ark and Abraham left his home, you must take steps in accordance with your faith. This might mean making decisions that align with your trust in God's provision, health, guidance, or protection, even if you cannot yet see the result.

Expect to See Results

Faith expects the invisible to become visible. Just as you would wait for the construction of a building once its foundation is laid, expect God to bring about what you have believed for. Your faith is the assurance that what you hope for will materialize, just as the blueprint of a building is made into reality with time and effort.

Persevere in Faith

Often, there may be a waiting period between the moment you exercise faith and the time you see the manifestation. During this time, stand firm in your belief. Your faith is not futile—it is working in the unseen realm to bring about the things you hope for.

Conclusion: Faith—A Tangible Substance That Transforms Reality

Hebrews 11:1 reveals faith as far more than just a philosophical or mystical idea. Faith is a tangible substance, the very foundation of our hopes and the evidence of God's promises, even when they are not yet visible. When we live by faith, we engage with the unseen, knowing that God will bring our hopes into reality. By aligning our actions with our faith, we participate in the divine process that transforms the invisible into the visible.

Faith, in this sense, becomes a spiritual force that affects our lives, circumstances, and the world around us. It is not a passive or theoretical concept, but a powerful, tangible substance that brings God's promises into being. When we embrace faith in this way, we can confidently walk through life, knowing that we are not just hoping in something uncertain, but standing firm on the solid foundation of God's Word, certain that the invisible will become visible in His perfect timing.

The Reward of Faithful Giving

Abel's legacy reminds us that God sees the heart behind the gift. His offering was accepted because it was given by faith, and God "spoke well of his offerings." This divine commendation reveals that God is pleased when we give in faith.

> **Malachi 3:10**
>
> *"Bring the whole tithe into the storehouse, that there may be food in my house. Test me in this," says the Lord Almighty, "and see if I will not throw open the floodgates of heaven and pour out so much blessing that there will not be room enough to store it."*

The reward of faithful tithing is not just material blessing but the assurance of God's favor and provision.

Abel's faith still speaks today, calling us to trust God fully and honor Him with our best.

In fact, God is so determined that Tithing is an act of giving in your life, He makes a promise to you, saying, "Test me in this…"

The Principle of The First

Genesis 14:18
Then Melchizedek, king of Salem, brought out bread and wine. He was priest of God Most High, and he blessed Abram, saying, "Blessed be Abram by God Most High, Creator of heaven and earth. And praise be to God Most High, who delivered your enemies into your hand." Then Abram gave him a tenth of everything.

Abram practiced Tithing.

Abram used his household servants, who were well-trained for battle, to rescue five kings. It was customary that when you won a battle, the spoils of war became the possessions of the victor.

After delivering the kings from defeat, Abram approached Melchizedek, the Priest. This figure is crucial in understanding the Tithe.

Before Abram divided up the spoils, he set aside the Tithe as the First.

Rather than keep the spoils, Abram refused, saying, "With the raised hand, I have sworn an oath to the Lord, God Most High, Creator of heaven and earth, that I will accept nothing belonging to you, not even a thread or the strap of a sandal so that you will never be able to say, 'I made Abram rich.'

Tithing is not just an act of generosity or financial strategy; it is an expression of alignment with a divine principle woven throughout history. The Principle of the First is one of the most powerful and transformative aspects of tithing. It speaks to the very heart of our faith, our priorities, and our trust in the provision of God.

The concept of giving the "first" and "best" portion of our resources is not a new idea. It has deep roots in the biblical narrative and spiritual practice, shaping how we approach God and our wealth. This chapter will explore the historical, biblical, and psychological significance of this principle and why it matters in the practice of tithing.

Historical and Biblical Insights into the 'First Fruits'

Giving the first portion of our harvest, wealth, or income is foundational to Jewish and Christian faiths. It is deeply embedded in the concept of "first fruits" found throughout the Bible. The "first fruits" refer to the initial portion of a harvest or increase offered to God as an act of worship, gratitude, and trust in His continued provision.

The principle of the first fruits is established as a law in the Old Testament in the book of Exodus.

> **Exodus 23:19**
> *"The first of the firstfruits of your land you shall bring into the house of the Lord your God."*

This offering was symbolic of the whole harvest being given to God, acknowledging that everything originated with Him and that the first and best portion should be returned to Him in worship.

This practice is not limited to produce or livestock but also extends to finances.

Leviticus 27:30
"The tenth of the land, whether of the seed of the land or of the fruit of the trees, is the Lord's."

This tithe was to be the first of the produce, and the Israelites were commanded to bring it to God as a sign of their obedience and faith in His provision.

But why the **first** portion? Why does it matter that we give the first rather than the last or a portion left over after everything else has been taken care of?

The answer lies in the deep spiritual significance of putting God first in our lives. The first portion is not just a token offering but a powerful declaration that God is our source and provider. It is an act of faith that acknowledges that God is the one who blesses and sustains us, and by giving the first, we are honoring His place in our lives.

Matthew 6:33

"But seek first his kingdom and his righteousness, and all these things will be given to you as well."

While everyone else seeks clothes, cars, and cottages, the man who seeks God demonstrates it with the Tithe.

In the book of Proverbs, we read, *"Honor the Lord with your wealth, with the firstfruits of all your crops; then your barns will be filled to overflowing, and your vats will brim over with new wine"* (Proverbs 3:9-10). This passage makes it clear that when we give God the first of our wealth, He responds by blessing us abundantly.

The Psychological and Spiritual Impact of Giving the First and Best

Giving the first and best portion is not just about obedience or fulfilling a command; it has profound psychological and spiritual effects. When we give God the first of what we have, we are making a statement about what we truly value. We are choosing to place Him above all else, even above our own needs and desires.

This act of prioritization does something deep within us. It shifts our perspective on wealth and resources. We no longer see our income or possessions solely for our benefit but as gifts entrusted to us by God. This shift in mindset leads to a deep sense of gratitude and humility. We begin to see ourselves as stewards of everything in our lives.

Psychologically, the act of giving the first portion also has a profound effect on our relationship with fear and anxiety.

Matthew 6:34

Therefore do not worry about tomorrow, for

tomorrow will worry about itself. Each day has enough trouble of its own.

Many people fear scarcity, especially when it comes to money. The instinct is often to hold tightly to what we have, especially when we feel uncertain about the future.

However, when we give the first portion—before we see how the rest of our needs will be met— we are expressing a deep trust in God's faithfulness.

We are saying, "I trust You, God, to meet all of my needs, even before I see how You will do it."

This trust is not passive but active. It is a faith that requires us to step out of our comfort zone and choose to believe that God will provide.

In Matthew 6:33, Jesus instructs us, *"But seek first His kingdom and His righteousness, and all these things will be given to you as well."*

The principle of the first is an embodiment of this command. When we seek God's kingdom first, we acknowledge that He is our priority, and in doing so, we trust He will provide for every other need.

Spiritually, the impact of giving the first portion of our wealth is transformative.

Romans 12:2

Do not conform to the pattern of this world, but be transformed by the renewing of your mind. Then you will be able to test and approve what God's will is—his good, pleasing and perfect will.

Tithing aligns our hearts with God's priorities. It breaks the power that money can have over us and frees us to live generously, trusting that God will provide. As we give the first, we are reminded that God is the ultimate giver. He gave His Son as the first and best offering for our salvation. When we give the first of our wealth, we participate in God's character—generous, sacrificial, and abundant.

Moreover, giving the first fruits establishes a rhythm of gratitude and worship. By consistently giving the first portion, we build a lifestyle of prioritizing God above all else. This practice creates a constant reminder that He is the source of all good things. The cycle of giving and receiving reinforces a deep connection between our hearts and His provision.

The Power of First Things in Everyday Life

The principle of the first is not limited to tithing alone. It applies to all areas of our lives. In our time, energy, and talents, giving the first to God can bring about profound transformation. Whether it's the first moments of our day spent in prayer or the first decision we make in a financial transaction, prioritizing God in these small moments leads to a life marked by peace, abundance, and purpose.

There is power in putting God first. It reorders our priorities and invites Him to lead every area of our lives. When we choose to give God the first of what we have, we are creating space for Him to move in powerful ways, both spiritually and practically.

The Principle of the First is an act of faith. It is putting faith into action. In fact, as Abel demonstrated, Tithing is the first act of faith.

The Test of Obedience

Malachi 3:10

"Bring the whole tithe into the storehouse, that there may be food in my house. Test me in this," says the Lord Almighty, "and see if I will not throw open the floodgates of heaven and pour out so much blessing that there will not be room enough to store it."

The Tithe is far more than a financial obligation —it is an expression of the heart worshiping God. From the earliest days of humanity, as seen in the story of Abel, giving has been an act of faith and reverence toward God. However, over time, the Israelites began to neglect this sacred practice, prompting God to establish the tithe in the Levitical law.

In Malachi 3:10, God challenges His people:

"Bring the whole tithe into the storehouse, that there may be food in my house. Test me in this," says the Lord Almighty, "and see if I will not throw open the floodgates of heaven and pour out so much blessing that there will not be room enough to store it."

This verse highlights the tension between the Israelites' disobedience and God's desire to bless them. While the law served as a framework to guide their giving, God's ultimate purpose was to draw His people into a heart-centered relationship where giving was an act of worship, not mere compliance.

When the heart is absent, the Law is required.

Tithing: A Matter of Worship, Not Just Law

Hebrews 7:1-10 provides a profound contrast between tithing as a legal requirement and tithing as an act of worship. This passage refers to Abraham giving a tithe to Melchizedek, a priest of the Most High God. This moment occurred long before the establishment of the Levitical law, demonstrating that tithing is rooted in faith and relationship with God, not legal obligation.

Key Points from Hebrews 7

- **Abraham's Tithe to Melchizedek**
  Abraham gave a tenth of the spoils to Melchizedek after his victory in battle. This act was spontaneous and voluntary, rooted in gratitude and reverence for God's provision and blessing. It was not mandated by law but inspired by worship.

- **A Higher Priesthood**
  Melchizedek's priesthood is described as eternal, foreshadowing Christ's role as our High Priest. This shows that Tithing transcends the Levitical system, aligning with the eternal order established by Christ.

- **The Superiority of Worship Over Obligation**
  The passage emphasizes that Levi, through Abraham, effectively paid Tithes to Melchizedek, showing that the principle of Tithing is greater than the Levitical law. It originates from a heart of honor and faith, not mere duty.

The Israelites' Failure: A Heart Issue

The Israelites' neglect of the Tithe, as addressed in Malachi 3:8-10, was not just disobedience to a law—it revealed a deeper problem of the heart.

They failed to honor God as their Provider and Sustainer. Instead of bringing the first and best, they withheld, prioritizing their own needs, cravings, and desires over worshiping God.

God instituted the Tithe in the law not to burden His people but to teach them dependence, trust, and reverence.

It was a test of obedience designed to draw their hearts back to Him. However, over time, many reduced Tithing to a legalistic practice, missing its true purpose as an act of worship.

Many people today are giving as Cain gave, a token or a tip rather than the Tithe.

You tip the one who serves you;
you Tithe to the One whom you serve.

The Heart of Worship in Tithing

Tithing as worship requires a shift from obligation to devotion. It is not about fulfilling a rule but about expressing love, gratitude, and trust in God.

Key Contrasts Between Worship and Law in Tithing:

Motivation

Under the Law, Tithing was often seen as an obligation to avoid punishment. As worship, Tithing flows from a heart that desires to honor God for who He is and what He has done.

Perspective

Under the Law, Tithing was a transaction—something given to fulfill a requirement. As worship, Tithing is relational—an offering that acknowledges God as the source of all blessings.

Faith

Under the Law, obedience to the Tithe could be devoid of faith, done out of routine. As worship, faith is central, trusting God to provide and bless in response to giving.

The Test of Obedience Today

Even today, Tithing serves as a test of obedience, revealing where our hearts are. You've heard this a thousand times: God does not need our money, but He desires our hearts. Money represents you. It is the accumulation of your time, energy, work, creativity, and labor. You are simply using money as the currency to express the intangible commodities.

The act of bringing the first 10% of our income to Him is a declaration that He is first in our lives.

Practical Steps to Tithe as Worship

1. **Start with the Heart**
    Before giving, examine your motives. Are you tithing out of obligation or as an act of gratitude and faith?
2. **Honor God First**
    The principle of the firstfruits remains significant. Give the first and best portion of your income, trusting God with the rest.

3. **Trust His Promises**

   Meditate on Scriptures like Malachi 3:10 and 2 Corinthians 9:8, which remind us that God is faithful to bless those who give cheerfully and sacrificially.

4. **Be Consistent**

   Worship requires consistency. Make tithing a regular part of your spiritual discipline, reflecting your ongoing trust in God.

Christ and the Heart of Giving

In Christ, we are no longer bound by the law, but the principles of Tithing remain relevant as a means of worship.

Jesus affirmed this in Matthew 23:23, where He rebuked the Pharisees for neglecting justice, mercy, and faithfulness while meticulously Tithing. His words remind us that tithing should never be reduced to legalism but must flow from a heart aligned with God's purposes.

Under the New Covenant, Christ's sacrifice fulfills and transcends the law. As believers, we are called to give generously and sacrificially, reflecting the heart of worship Abel exhibited and Abraham demonstrated to Melchizedek.

Worshiping with the Tithe and Communion: The Role of Melchizedek and Jesus as Our High Priest

The act of worship is central to our Christian faith. It is an offering of our hearts, lives, and all that we have to honor God.

To understand the deep significance of worship through Tithing, let's look to the example of Melchizedek, the priest-king, and the ultimate fulfillment of that priesthood in Jesus Christ, our High Priest.

The Encounter with Melchizedek: A Type of Christ

After Abel honored the LORD with the Tithe, the second instance of tithing in the Bible occurs in Genesis 14, where Abraham, after a victorious battle, meets Melchizedek, the King of Salem.

Melchizedek is described as both a king and a priest of God Most High. He blesses Abraham, saying, "Blessed be Abram of God Most High, Possessor of heaven and earth; and blessed be God Most High, Who has delivered your enemies into your hand."

In response to this blessing, Abraham gives Melchizedek a tithe of all he had obtained from the battle.

Melchizedek's encounter with Abraham is significant because it foreshadows the priesthood of Jesus Christ.

The Prince of Peace, Melchizedek, brings out the Bread and the Wine and speaks the Blessing when Abram approaches Him with the Tithe.

Hebrews 7:1-3 speaks of Melchizedek as a "type" of Christ, saying that he was "without father, without mother, without genealogy," and that he was "made like the Son of God."

In this mysterious figure, we see a shadow of the eternal, unchanging priesthood of Jesus. The giving of and worship with the Tithe in this encounter is not simply a financial transaction; it is a spiritual act of worship, recognizing God's sovereignty over all things and acknowledging Him as the ultimate source of victory and provision.

Worshiping with the Tithe: Honoring God's Sovereignty

When we give our tithe, we are participating in an act of worship that acknowledges God's sovereignty over every area of our lives. Just as Abraham recognized the greatness of Melchizedek and gave a tenth of his spoils in gratitude for God's deliverance, we too offer our Tithe as a recognition of God's provision, sovereignty, and faithfulness in our lives.

The Tithe is not a transaction based on obligation but an offering that expresses our trust in God. It is an act of worship that acknowledges that everything we have is a gift from God, and we give a portion back to Him in honor of His role as the ultimate Provider. This act of worship aligns us with God's kingdom, placing our trust in His provision rather than our own abilities or efforts.

Jesus as Our High Priest: The Fulfillment of the Melchizedek Priesthood

In the New Testament, Jesus is revealed as the fulfillment of the Melchizedek priesthood. In Hebrews 7:23-28, the writer contrasts the Levitical priesthood, which was based on descendants and sacrifices, with the eternal priesthood of Jesus, who, like Melchizedek, is a priest forever. Jesus' priesthood is not based on genealogy or lineage but on His divine nature, His sacrifice, and His eternal role as the intercessor between God and humanity.

Jesus, as the High Priest, mediates a new covenant for us. Unlike the priests of the Old Testament who had to offer repeated sacrifices for sin, Jesus offered Himself as the once-for-all sacrifice for sin. His priesthood is not temporal or earthly but eternal. Through Jesus, we are able to enter into the presence of God and offer ourselves as living sacrifices, holy and acceptable to Him.

The act of Tithing, when understood in the light of Jesus' priesthood, is an act of worship that acknowledges Jesus' authority and mediation as the High Priest. By giving our tithe, we are recognizing that our lives, our finances, and all that we have belong to Him, and we honor Him by giving back a portion of what He has entrusted to us.

The Communion Connection: Partaking of Christ's Body and Blood

The practice of communion (or the Lord's Supper) is another vital expression of worship. Jesus instituted this sacrament during the Last Supper with His disciples, instructing them to eat the bread, representing His body, and drink the wine, representing His blood, in remembrance of Him (Luke 22:19-20). Communion is an act of worship that celebrates Jesus' sacrifice and His establishment of the new covenant.

In the context of Tithing, communion can be seen as a parallel act of worship. Just as we partake of the bread and wine to remember Jesus' sacrifice and to enter into fellowship with Him, we offer the tithe as an act of remembrance and gratitude for all that God has provided. Communion symbolizes our union with Christ and the blessings we receive from His sacrifice.

Similarly, tithing symbolizes our union with Christ in His kingdom, and through the Tithe, we acknowledge that all things come from Him and that we are called to steward His blessings wisely.

Worshiping through Both Tithe and Communion: A Holistic Act of Honor

Tithing and communion both serve as acts of worship that bring us closer to God, aligning our hearts with His purposes. They are both opportunities to honor God with our lives—our resources in the case of tithing and our hearts and bodies in the case of communion. Through both, we recognize that everything we have comes from God and that He is worthy of our worship, our devotion, and our obedience.

In worshiping with the tithe, we participate in a divine exchange: we offer our resources, and God responds by opening the windows of heaven, pouring out blessings upon us. Similarly, in communion, we receive the body and blood of Christ, participating in the covenant of grace and eternal life that He has established through His sacrifice. Both acts of worship remind us of God's faithfulness and goodness and invite us to engage in His divine economy, where the physical and the spiritual intersect.

A Life of Worship in Spirit and Truth

Worshiping with the Tithe and participating in communion are both acts of faith and obedience. They point to the greater reality of our relationship with God, made possible through the eternal priesthood of Jesus.
Just as Melchizedek's blessing of Abraham foreshadowed the priestly work of Christ, so too does our practice of Tithing and communion serve as a powerful acknowledgment of Jesus' role as our High Priest.

Both of these practices invite us into a deeper fellowship with God, acknowledging His provision, His sacrifice, and His eternal reign.

In Tithing, we worship God with our finances, acknowledging His sovereignty over all we have. In communion, we worship God with our hearts, recognizing His ultimate sacrifice for our salvation. Together, they form a holistic expression of worship, where we honor God in both the material and spiritual realms, offering ourselves wholly to Him in gratitude and devotion.

The Window: Portal to the Unseen

Malachi 3:10

"Bring the whole tithe into the storehouse, that there may be food in my house. Test me in this," says the Lord Almighty, "and see if I will not throw open the windows of heaven and pour out so much blessing that there will not be room enough to store it."

The phrase "windows of heaven" is often understood as an image of God opening the heavens to pour out blessings, but the original Hebrew word for "windows" offers a deeper insight. The word used, "***arubbah***" (אֲרֻבָּה), carries the idea of a network or lattice—an interconnected system of openings through which provision flows.

This concept is life-changing when you realize what is happening when you Tithe.

The Network of Heaven and the Internet Protocol: A Comparison

Today, we are accustomed to connecting to the internet using devices like smartphones and tablets. With the touch of a button, we have access to the vast expanse of human knowledge, culture, commerce, and communication that the internet provides. The internet operates through a set of protocols, rules that allow devices to connect, communicate, and share information across the globe.

In a similar way, the network of heaven operates through divine protocols that allow believers to access God's limitless provision, wisdom, and blessings.

Let's explore this analogy and see how the "window" to heaven and the "internet protocol" can provide us a deeper understanding of how heaven's network works.

The Window of Heaven: A Spiritual Portal

In Malachi 3:10, God speaks of "opening the windows of heaven" as a response to those who faithfully Tithe. This is not just a metaphorical phrase but a representation of a spiritual portal through which divine blessings flow into the lives of those who honor God. When the "window of heaven" is opened, it allows access to a realm beyond our physical understanding—the unseen realm where God's provision, wisdom, and favor are waiting to be poured out.

Just as the internet functions through a specific connection protocol, the window of heaven operates through a spiritual protocol.

Tithing, faith, obedience, and prayer are the key spiritual practices that allow you to access this divine network. This network is not limited by geographical distance, but reaches wherever the believer is, ready to provide what is needed according to God's will.

The Internet Protocol: A Connection to the Digital World

The internet, like the network of heaven, operates through protocols—the rules and standards that guide how data is sent, received, and processed. These protocols, such as TCP/IP (Transmission Control Protocol/Internet Protocol), allow different devices and systems to communicate and share information seamlessly. When you type a URL into a browser or open an app, your device sends a request through this protocol to access data stored on remote servers, enabling you to view a webpage or stream a video.

In the same way, the "protocols" of heaven guide how we connect with God's network. The ultimate "protocol" is Jesus Christ, who, as the Mediator, allows us to access God's kingdom and resources.

Through faith in Jesus, we are granted the ability to pray, seek God's wisdom, and enter into His presence. Each act of worship, prayer, or obedience is like sending a request to heaven, expecting a response from God, just as a device sends a request over the internet.

Accessing the Unseen Realm: The Role of Faith

Just as we rely on devices like smartphones or tablets to access the internet, in the same way, we rely on our spiritual devices—our hearts and faith—to access the network of heaven.

We don't see the "connection" or "data flow" in the same way we see the glowing screen of a device, but we trust in it because we experience the results. When we Tithe, pray, and obey God's word, we are connecting to heaven's network. We may not see it with our natural eyes, but by faith, we understand that we are receiving the blessings, guidance, and answers that God has promised.

The internet is always available as long as we have the right connection, just as heaven's network is always accessible when we walk in the ways that honor God. It's not limited by time or space; God is always available to us. But to truly access this network, we must align ourselves with God's will and trust the divine protocol that He has established.

The Purpose of the Network: Sharing Information and Resources

The internet was created to share information. It connects people across continents, allowing them to communicate, share knowledge, and collaborate in ways that were once unimaginable. The network of heaven functions in a similar way —its purpose is to share divine wisdom, provision, and blessings with those who seek God's will. Just as the internet allows you to access vast amounts of information for your personal and professional growth, heaven's network gives you access to eternal wisdom, ideas, strategies, and favor to fulfill your purpose on earth.

The difference is that while the internet shares human knowledge, heaven's network shares *divine* knowledge. It offers wisdom that surpasses understanding, provision that exceeds need, and a peace that transcends circumstances.

When you are connected to heaven's network, you are not just accessing information; you are receiving the very resources and favor needed to fulfill God's calling in your life.

The Power of Connection: Transforming Lives

Just as the internet has revolutionized communication, business, and education, the network of heaven has the power to transform lives. Access to the internet has allowed individuals and businesses to grow and connect in ways that would have once been impossible.

Similarly, when we tap into the window of heaven, we experience a transformation that affects every aspect of our lives.

When we connect to Heaven's network, our personal lives, families, work, and communities can be radically changed. God's blessings, wisdom, and provision flow through this connection, enabling us to fulfill our purposes on earth and change the world around us. The difference lies in the source: the internet connects us to human knowledge, while heaven's network connects us to the divine wisdom of the Creator.

Using the Window: Faithful Giving and Prayers

One of the primary ways to open the window of heaven is through faithful giving, specifically through the act of Tithing.

Tithing is a key practice that aligns us with God's kingdom and opens up the flow of blessings into our lives. Just as clicking a link or making a request on the internet opens up access to desired content, giving and obeying God's commands unlocks the treasures stored in heaven.

Prayer, worship, and living a life of obedience also serve as requests to God that bring us into connection with His eternal network. These practices act like requests sent through the protocol of faith, and in return, we receive divine insights, favor, and the provision to accomplish our mission on earth.

Accessing the Unseen Network

In both the physical and spiritual realms, access to networks requires the right tools, understanding of protocols, and the trust that the system works. Just as the internet allows us to access knowledge and connect with others, the network of heaven allows us to access divine resources and wisdom to fulfill our purpose on earth. Through the spiritual protocol of faith—through tithing, obedience, and prayer—we can open the window of heaven and receive all that God has prepared for us.

Just like the internet, heaven's network is always available to us. All we need to do is trust in the divine protocol, open our hearts to the connection, and watch as God's blessings flow into every area of our lives.

Similarly, the Greek word "***anastomosis***" (ἀναστόμωσις), which refers to the joining or interconnection of vessels, enriches our understanding of how giving activates divine provision. Together, these concepts reveal that tithing is not merely a transaction but a spiritual key that opens the interconnected channels of heaven, allowing God's blessings to flow into every area of our lives.

The Hebrew Concept: Arubbah (Windows as a Network)

In ancient Hebrew thought, ***arubbah*** was more than just an ordinary window. It referred to an aperture or lattice-like structure, often part of a more extensive system designed for airflow or access. This network imagery suggests that the windows of heaven are not isolated points of blessing but an interconnected framework through which God channels His provision.

When God promises to "open the windows of heaven" in Malachi 3:10, He is describing the activation of a heavenly network—a divine system that links His resources with the needs of His people. This network operates in response to our faith and obedience, specifically through tithing.

The Greek Concept: Anastomosis (Interconnected Flow)

The Greek word ***anastomosis*** adds another layer to this understanding. Used in medicine to describe the connection of blood vessels, it denotes a network where life-giving blood flows freely between pathways. This interconnected system ensures that every part of the body receives nourishment and sustenance.

It is also a concept used in the new field of artificial intelligence, neural networks, and deep learning.

When applied to the principle of Tithing, anastomosis illustrates how our obedience creates openings in the spiritual realm, allowing God's blessings to flow seamlessly into our lives. Just as interconnected vessels sustain the body, the heavenly network sustains us spiritually, emotionally, and materially.

The Heavenly Network in Action

When we Tithe, we activate this divine network. Our giving is not just a singular act but a connection point that links us to the resources of heaven.

God as the Source

The heavenly network begins with God, who is the ultimate source of all blessings. Psalm 24:1 reminds us, "The earth is the Lord's, and everything in it." By tithing, we acknowledge God as the Provider and connect to His inexhaustible supply.

Faith as the Connector

Tithing requires faith, which acts as the conduit for God's blessings. Hebrews 11:6 states, "Without faith it is impossible to please God." Through faith, we trust that God will open the interconnected windows of heaven and meet our needs according to His riches in glory (Philippians 4:19).

The Flow of Blessing

Once the network is activated, God's blessings begin to flow. These blessings are not limited to finances; they encompass every area of life— peace, protection, health, relationships, and spiritual growth. Just as anastomosis ensures that blood reaches every part of the body, the heavenly network ensures that God's provision reaches every part of our lives.

Tithing and the Opening of Heaven

In Malachi 3:10, God explicitly links tithing to the opening of heaven:

> *"Test me in this," says the Lord Almighty, "and see if I will not throw open the windows of heaven and pour out so much blessing that there will not be room enough to store it."*

This promise reveals three key truths about the heavenly network:

1. Tithing Creates an Opening
Our obedience in tithing unlocks the network, allowing the flow of God's provision. Without this act of faith, the windows remain closed, and the blessings are withheld.

2. The Flow is Abundant
God promises to pour out a blessing so great that it cannot be contained. This reflects the infinite nature of His resources and His desire to bless His people abundantly.

3. The Network Operates on Faith and Obedience

The heavenly network is not activated by need but by obedience. When we honor God with the firstfruits of our income, we demonstrate our trust in His ability to provide, thereby opening the channels of His blessing.

Practical Application: Living Within the Heavenly Network

To fully experience the flow of blessings through the heavenly network, we must align our lives with its principles:

- **Tithe Faithfully**
  Commit to giving the first 10% of your income to God. This act of faith activates the network and establishes a connection to His provision.
- **Trust God's Timing**
  The flow of blessings may not always align with our expectations, but God's timing is perfect. Trust that He will meet your needs at the right time and in the right way.

- **Recognize the Multiplicity of Blessings**
  The blessings that flow through the heavenly network are not limited to finances. Look for God's provision in relationships, opportunities, health, and peace.
- **Stay Connected Through Gratitude**
  Gratitude keeps the network flowing. Acknowledge and thank God for every blessing, big or small, recognizing His hand in all areas of your life.
- **Be a Conduit of Blessing**
  Just as the heavenly network flows to you, it should flow through you. Use your resources to bless others, extending the reach of God's provision.

The heavenly network is a divine system established by God to meet the needs of His people. Through the Hebrew concept of ***arubbah*** and the Greek understanding of ***anastomosis***, we see that this network operates as an interconnected flow of blessings, activated by faith and obedience.

When we tithe, we engage this network, opening the windows of heaven and allowing God's abundant provision to pour into our lives. As we remain faithful and connected to the Source, we not only experience His blessings but also become channels of His goodness to the world.

Tithing is not just about finances—it is about participating in the heavenly network, trusting God as our Provider, and living in the overflow of His limitless grace.

Jacob's Encounter with the Open Heaven: A Revelation of Tithing and Access to the Unseen Realm

Jacob's encounter at Bethel is one of the most vivid biblical illustrations of the open heaven. This divine experience unveils the profound connection between faith, obedience, and access to the unseen spiritual realm.

Found in Genesis 28:10-22, Jacob's dream reveals a heavenly network where God's blessings flow freely, affirming the principle that tithing opens access to the resources and presence of heaven.

Jacob's Journey to Bethel

Fleeing from his brother Esau, Jacob found himself in an unfamiliar wilderness. As he lay down to sleep with a stone for a pillow, he experienced a supernatural vision:

"He had a dream in which he saw a stairway resting on the earth, with its top reaching to heaven, and the angels of God were ascending and descending on it. There above it stood the Lord, and he said: 'I am the Lord, the God of your father Abraham and the God of Isaac. I will give you and your descendants the land on which you are lying.'" (Genesis 28:12-13)

This stairway, often referred to as "Jacob's Ladder," represents the open heaven—a direct connection between the earthly and heavenly realms. The angels ascending and descending symbolize the flow of divine activity, while God's presence at the top affirms His sovereignty over this exchange.

The Tithe as a Response to Open Heaven

When Jacob awoke, he recognized the significance of this encounter:

"Surely the Lord is in this place, and I was not aware of it... This is none other than the house

of God; this is the gate of heaven." (Genesis 28:16-17)

In awe of God's presence and the promise of His provision, Jacob made a covenant:

"Then Jacob made a vow, saying, 'If God will be with me and will watch over me on this journey I am taking and will give me food to eat and clothes to wear... then the Lord will be my God... and of all that you give me I will give you a tenth.'" (Genesis 28:20-22)

Jacob's promise to Tithe reflects his recognition of the divine principle: the Tithe is an act of worship and a response to God's open heaven. By giving a tenth of his income, Jacob acknowledged God as his Provider and aligned himself with the flow of heavenly blessings.

The Open Heaven and Access to the Unseen Realm

Jacob's vision reveals three critical aspects of how tithing gives us access to the unseen realm:

1. **A Divine Connection**
   The stairway signifies the connection

between heaven and earth. Through the Tithe, believers establish a spiritual link to God's provision, activating the flow of His blessings into their lives. This connection is not merely transactional but relational, grounded in trust and faith.

2. **Angelic Activity**
   The angels ascending and descending reflect the unseen activity of heaven on behalf of God's people. Tithing invites divine intervention, releasing the resources, protection, and guidance necessary for life's journey.

3. **God's Presence and Promise**
   At the heart of Jacob's encounter is God's presence, who reaffirms His covenant with Abraham and Isaac. Tithing aligns us with God's promises, opening the unseen realm where His plans and purposes are revealed.

Practical Application: Living Under the Open Heaven

Jacob's experience at Bethel offers timeless lessons for believers today:

- **Recognize God's Presence**
  Like Jacob, we must cultivate awareness of God's presence in every aspect of our lives. Tithing is an act of faith that acknowledges His provision and invites His activity into our circumstances.
- **Establish a Covenant**
  Jacob's vow to tithe demonstrates his commitment to honoring God. By faithfully giving the firstfruits of our income, we establish a covenant that aligns us with the flow of heavenly blessings.
- **Expect Divine Provision**
  The open heaven is a promise of God's abundant provision. Through tithing, we access the unseen realm where God's resources are limitless, and His faithfulness is unwavering.

Jacob's encounter at Bethel reveals the profound truth that tithing gives us access to the open heaven. This act of faith connects us to a divine network where God's blessings flow freely, empowering us to live in the fullness of His provision and purpose.

Just as Jacob responded to the open heaven with worship and a vow to tithe, we too can step into the unseen realm through obedience and faith. By honoring God with the firstfruits of our income, we align ourselves with His promises and experience the transformative power of living under the open heaven.

Tithe

The Economics of Heaven

Luke 6:38

"Give, and it will be given to you. A good measure, pressed down, shaken together and running over, will be poured into your lap. For with the measure you use, it will be measured to you."

Understanding God's Divine Economy Through Tithing

God's economy operates on principles that transcend the natural systems of this world. While earthly economies are built on scarcity, competition, and self-interest, the divine economy is grounded in abundance, generosity, and multiplication. Tithing is a vital key to unlocking the resources of God's economy, as it aligns us with His supernatural principles of provision and prosperity.

The Principle of Divine Ownership

At the heart of God's economy is the understanding that everything originates with Him:

> *"The earth is the Lord's, and everything in it, the world, and all who live in it." (Psalm 24:1)*

Tithing is an acknowledgment of God's ownership.

When we give the first tenth of our income to Him, we demonstrate our trust in His ability to multiply and provide beyond what earthly systems can achieve. It is a recognition that God, not money or human effort, is the ultimate Source of all provision.

Heaven's Currencies: God's Means of Exchange

In earthly economies, money serves as the primary medium of exchange. But in the divine economy, God's currencies include wisdom, ideas, concepts, inventions, work, and intellectual properties. These intangible resources are far more powerful than earthly wealth, as they have

the potential to create lasting impact and
generational blessings.

- **Wisdom**
  God's wisdom unlocks strategies for success
  that surpass human understanding. Solomon's
  wealth, for instance, was rooted in the wisdom
  God gave him. (1 Kings 3:12-13)
- **Ideas and Concepts**
  Divine ideas often lead to innovations that
  transform industries and communities.
  Consider Joseph in Egypt. God's insight into
  managing famine brought prosperity to an
  entire nation. (Genesis 41:33-36)
- **Inventions**
  God-inspired creativity leads to breakthroughs
  that benefit humanity. These inventions often
  originate from people who dedicate their work
  and resources to His kingdom.
- **Work and Diligence**
  God blesses the work of our hands when we
  labor with integrity and faithfulness.
  (Deuteronomy 28:12)
- **Intellectual Properties**
  God gives His people the capacity to create
  systems, content, and innovations that
  generate ongoing provision and influence.

The Multiplication Principle in God's Economy

God's economy operates on the principle of multiplication. Unlike the earthly model of addition or linear growth, God takes what is surrendered to Him and multiplies it exponentially.

The Widow's Oil

In 2 Kings 4:1-7, a widow obeyed the prophet Elisha's instruction to pour out her last bit of oil into borrowed jars. As she poured, the oil multiplied until every jar was filled, providing more than enough to meet her needs.

The Feeding of the 5,000

In Matthew 14:13-21, Jesus multiplied five loaves and two fish to feed thousands. This miracle demonstrates that when placed in God's hands, even the smallest offering can become abundant provision.

The Seed and the Harvest

Jesus taught that a single seed planted in faith can yield a bountiful harvest: "Give, and it will be given to you. A good measure, pressed down, shaken together and running over, will be poured into your lap." (Luke 6:38)

Tithing: The Gateway to God's Economy

Tithing is not a transaction; it is a covenantal act of worship that connects us to God's economy. When we tithe, we:

- **Acknowledge God as Provider**
  By giving the firstfruits, we affirm our trust in God to meet our needs and multiply what remains.
- **Align with Kingdom Principles**
  Tithing places us under God's divine order, where provision flows freely according to His promises.
- **Activate Heaven's Resources**
  Malachi 3:10 declares that tithing opens the windows of heaven, allowing blessings to pour into our lives. These blessings often manifest as wisdom, favor, and opportunities that earthly

standards cannot measure; however, they can be converted into earthly currencies.

How Heaven's Economy Differs from Earthly Economies

EARTHLY ECONOMY	HEAVENLY ECONOMY
Scarcity *Limited resources*	**Abundance** *God owns everything*
Competition *Driven by self-interest*	**Cooperation** *Encourages generosity*
Linear Growth *Focused on addition*	**Multiplication** *Exponential increase*
Reliance on Human Effort	**Dependence on Divine Provision**
Temporary *Subject to fluctuation*	**Eternal** *Rooted in God's promises*

Practical Steps to Operate in God's Economy

1. **Tithe Faithfully**

   Commit to giving the first 10% of your

income to God, trusting Him to multiply and bless the remaining 90%.

2. **Sow Generously**
    Beyond the tithe, sow seeds of generosity into others' lives and ministries. God multiplies what is freely given in faith.

3. **Seek Divine Wisdom**
    Pray for wisdom and insight in managing resources, making decisions, and pursuing opportunities.

4. **Steward God's Currencies**
    Recognize and nurture the gifts God has given you—whether they are ideas, talents, or inventions. Dedicate these to His glory and expect Him to bring increase.

5. **Walk in Faith, Not Fear**
    Trust God's promises even when earthly circumstances seem uncertain. Remember, His economy is not subject to recessions, inflation, or market volatility.

God's divine economy is available to all who trust Him and align their lives with His principles.

Through Tithing, we enter a supernatural system where scarcity gives way to abundance, and provision flows from unexpected places.

As we sow into God's kingdom, we activate the currencies of heaven—wisdom, ideas, inventions, and more—unleashing their potential to create lasting impact. Tithing is not just an act of obedience; it is an invitation to participate in the limitless economy of heaven, where God multiplies what we surrender and meets every need according to His riches in glory.

"On Earth as It Is in Heaven": Tithing and Heaven's Network of Blessing

The phrase "on earth as it is in heaven" from the Lord's Prayer (Matthew 6:10) reveals God's desire to bring the fullness of His heavenly reality into our earthly experience. Heaven is a realm of abundance, divine order, and unbroken relationship with God. Tithing is one of the practical ways we align ourselves with this divine flow, opening the network of heaven's blessing to manifest in our daily lives.

The Heavenly Network of Provision

When we pray, "Your kingdom come, your will be done, on earth as it is in heaven," we are inviting God to establish His rule and provision in our lives. Tithing connects us to this heavenly network—a system where resources flow freely according to God's perfect will.

Heaven's Abundance

Heaven lacks nothing. Revelation 21 describes it as a place of unimaginable wealth and glory, where streets are paved with gold and gates are made of pearls. Tithing reflects our faith in this abundance, trusting that God's provision is limitless and accessible to us on earth.

The Open Heaven Promise

Remember, Malachi 3:10 speaks of God opening the windows of heaven to pour out blessings when we tithe. As we've learned the word "window" in Hebrew (אֲרוּבָּה, arubah) implies a network, a conduit through which heaven's resources flow into the earth. Tithing unlocks this divine network, allowing spiritual and material blessings to intersect with our earthly realities.

Practical Realities of "On Earth as It Is in Heaven"

When we tithe, we invite God to align our lives with heaven's order, transforming earthly circumstances to reflect His kingdom. Here's how this principle becomes a reality:

Provision for Every Need

In heaven, there is no lack. Tithing acknowledges God as our Provider, trusting Him to meet every need. This might manifest as financial provision, but it also includes opportunities, favor, and wisdom for life's challenges.

Divine Order and Protection

Heaven operates in perfect order, free from chaos or decay. Tithing brings our finances into alignment with God's kingdom principles, positioning us under His protection. Malachi 3:11 promises that God will rebuke the devourer on our behalf, ensuring that our resources are not wasted or destroyed.

Overflow of Blessing

Just as heaven is a place of overflowing joy and provision, tithing brings us into the realm of overflow. God not only meets our needs but also equips us to bless others, fulfilling His promise to make us channels of His generosity.

Living the Prayer Through Tithing

The Lord's Prayer invites us to align with Heaven's reality; Tithing is a tangible expression of this alignment. When we tithe, we declare:

"Our Father in heaven, hallowed be your name."—

Tithing is worship, honoring God as our source and sustainer.

"Your kingdom come, your will be done, on earth as it is in heaven."

Tithing invites God's kingdom principles to govern our finances and life.

"Give us today our daily bread."

Through tithing, we trust God to provide for our daily needs in abundance.

Experiencing Heaven on Earth

Tithing is not a mechanical obligation but an act of faith that opens the windows of heaven. It creates a conduit through which God's abundance flows into our lives, enabling us to experience the reality of "on earth as it is in heaven."

As we faithfully tithe, we activate a heavenly network that connects God's resources to our earthly needs. This alignment releases provision, protects our harvest, and empowers us to be a blessing to others. It is a partnership with God, transforming our natural circumstances into reflections of His supernatural kingdom.

The Network of Blessing: Learning to Profit

Isaiah 48:17

"This is what the Lord says—your Redeemer, the Holy One of Israel: 'I am the Lord your God, who teaches you what is best for you, who directs you in the way you should go.'"

Learning to Profit Under the Redeemer's Guidance

God is deeply invested in your success—not in a superficial sense of accumulating wealth, but in aligning your resources with your divine purpose.

True prosperity, as shown in Scripture, means having the means to fulfill your God-given meaning.

The Lord Jesus, our Redeemer, not only rescues us from sin but also leads us into a life where every step and every decision aligns with His will, ensuring that our journey goes well and that we profit in all that He calls us to do.

Prosperity is having the means to fulfill your meaning.

The Redeemer Who Teaches Us to Profit

The Hebrew word for "profit" (יָעַל, ya'al) in Isaiah 48:17 conveys the idea of advancing, thriving, and gaining benefit.

Jesus has a teaching on profit.

Jesus, as our Redeemer, teaches us how to live in spiritual, relational, and material prosperity by showing us the principles of divine provision. This doesn't simply mean financial gain; it includes wisdom, favor, opportunities, and everything needed to accomplish His purpose.

Prosperity with Purpose
God's guidance leads to holistic prosperity—provision for every need and the ability to fulfill

your calling. Prosperity is not an end in itself but a means to glorify God and serve others.

Guidance on the Journey

God directs us in the way we should go, illuminating the right paths at the right time. When we follow His instruction, even in uncertain circumstances, we experience His provision and peace.

Peter's Lesson on the Network of Blessing

One of the most vivid examples of the Lord teaching someone to profit is in Luke 5:1–7. Peter, a seasoned fisherman, was frustrated after a long night of catching nothing. Then Jesus, the Redeemer, gave him a simple but unexpected instruction:

Luke 5:4

"Put out into deep water, and let down the nets for a catch."

Peter could have relied on his own experience, doubted Jesus' unconventional advice, or dismissed the Redeemer's guidance altogether. But instead, he responded with faith:

Luke 5:5
"Master, we've worked hard all night and haven't caught anything. But because you say so, I will let down the nets."

The result? An overwhelming catch of fish, so abundant that the nets began to break, and they had to call for help to bring in the blessing.

Lessons from Peter's Experience

Peter's encounter reveals timeless truths about walking in the network of God's blessing:

Obedience Unlocks Provision
Even when Peter's logic and experience suggested otherwise, his obedience to Jesus' word positioned him to receive an extraordinary blessing. God's instructions often defy human reasoning, but they lead to divine results.

Abundance Requires Community

The catch was so abundant that Peter needed help from others to bring it in. God's blessings are often meant to overflow, blessing others around us and creating a network of mutual support and generosity.

Faith Transcends Sight

Peter's decision to obey was rooted in faith. He trusted Jesus' word over his own understanding, stepping into a realm where heaven's provision became tangible on earth.

Walking in the Network of Blessing

Isaiah 48:17 reminds us that God's guidance is the key to living in the network of blessing. Jesus not only teaches us principles of provision but also invites us to participate in a divine economy where obedience, faith, and purpose intersect to produce abundance.

Seek His Guidance

Begin every decision, large or small, by seeking God's will. Through prayer and Scripture, ask for the Redeemer's direction, trusting that He will lead you in the way you should go.

Respond with Faith

When God gives an instruction, respond as Peter did: "Because You say so." Faith-filled obedience positions you to receive blessings you cannot achieve on your own.

Recognize the Purpose of Prosperity

Remember that prosperity is a means to fulfill God's purpose for your life. Whether it's financial provision, creative ideas, or opportunities, all blessings are meant to glorify Him and benefit others.

Trust in God's Timing

Just as Peter fished all night without success before Jesus intervened, there may be seasons of waiting or frustration. Trust that the Redeemer's guidance will come at the perfect time, bringing clarity and provision.

Your Will Be Done: Prosperity for His Glory

When we align with God's principles and trust the Redeemer's guidance, we step into a divine network of blessing where heaven's resources flow into our earthly lives. This is the essence of the prayer, "Your kingdom come, your will be done, on earth as it is in heaven."

The Lord teaches us to profit not for selfish gain but to fulfill His purposes and reflect His glory. Like Peter, we are called to obey, trust, and step into the deep, knowing that God's network of blessing is already in motion, ready to supply all we need to live lives of meaning, impact, and divine provision.

You will only prosper through connecting Heaven's will to Earth's frustration.

You Are Designed for a Purpose

You are not here by accident. You are uniquely designed, crafted with precision, and gifted with talents, insights, and abilities that no one else can replicate. You carry within you a piece of heaven's blueprint, a specific solution to an earthly problem, waiting to be revealed through your life.

Proverbs 20:5 (Amplified)
A plan (motive, wise counsel) in the heart of a man is like water in a deep well,
But a man of understanding draws it out.

Look around—there is frustration in the world, problems crying out for answers, and darkness longing for light. And here you are, with a unique combination of gifts and purpose, called to bring change, hope, and healing. Your life is the bridge between heaven's will and earth's need.

Think about it: no one else has your exact experiences, your precise perspective, or your divine assignment. God, in His infinite wisdom, placed you in this moment of history, in this place, with this design. You are here to make a difference.

You are not ordinary. You are extraordinary. The gifts you have are not just for you—they are meant to serve, to uplift, to transform. When you step into your purpose, aligning with God's plan, heaven's resources open to you. Wisdom, ideas, creativity, and provision flow through you like rivers to quench the thirst of a dry land.

Don't underestimate yourself. The problem you are meant to solve might seem overwhelming, but God has already equipped you with what you need. When you take the first step in faith, heaven responds. You are not alone—your Creator walks with you, empowering you every step of the way.

The world needs what you carry. Your unique design answers someone's prayer, the solution to a lingering challenge, the hope for a better tomorrow.

So rise up, take courage, and fulfill your purpose. Heaven is cheering you on, and the earth is waiting for you to shine.

Thou Shalt Prosper

I had the opportunity to meet Rabbi Daniel Lapin, a renowned author and speaker. I spent an hour talking to him about his book, **Thou Shalt Prosper**. I strongly encourage you to read it. He has a profound understanding of why the Jewish mindset of money has allowed the Jewish people to prosper.

Rabbi Daniel Lapin emphasizes the profound value of human and spiritual connections in achieving success and fulfillment. Rooted in ancient Jewish wisdom, his teachings highlight that relationships, not transactions or material wealth, are the true currency of prosperity. Rabbi Lapin often explains that the Hebrew language itself reflects the interconnected nature of life. For example, the Hebrew word for "life" (chai) is plural, signifying that life inherently involves connections with others.

Key Aspects of Rabbi Lapin's Teaching on Connections

Relationships as Assets

Rabbi Lapin teaches that cultivating strong relationships—family, friends, colleagues, and community—is essential for long-term success. These connections form a network of trust and reciprocity that can open doors, provide support, and amplify opportunities.

The Biblical Basis for Networking

Drawing on Jewish wisdom and biblical principles, he often cites examples like Joseph and Moses, who relied on their connections to fulfill their God-given missions. He explains that God created humans as relational beings, designed to thrive in community.

Business and Wealth Through Connection

Rabbi Lapin reframes the idea of wealth creation as a byproduct of serving others. He argues that business is fundamentally about solving problems for others and that the relationships you build are integral to creating value in the marketplace.

The Divine Conncction

Beyond human relationships, Rabbi Lapin underscores the importance of staying connected to God. He teaches that prayer, study, and acts of faith are essential for maintaining this spiritual connection, which brings clarity, wisdom, and purpose to all areas of life.

Hebrew Insights on Connection

Rabbi Lapin frequently explores the depth of Hebrew words to reveal their wisdom on connection. For instance, the Hebrew word for "blessing" (bracha) is tied to abundance and flow, suggesting that blessings often come through connections that allow resources and ideas to flow freely.

Giving as the Ultimate Connection

Rabbi Lapin teaches that giving—whether through charity, acts of kindness, or sharing wisdom—strengthens the fabric of relationships. Generosity not only benefits others but also enriches the giver by deepening their sense of purpose and belonging.

The Practical Takeaway

Rabbi Lapin's teaching on connections reminds us that success is rarely a solitary journey. By nurturing relationships with people and aligning with God's principles, individuals can build a life of abundance, service, and meaning. His work challenges the modern, often individualistic approach to success, encouraging a return to the timeless wisdom that prosperity grows through interdependence and connection.

Jesus Teaches Personal Capitalism

Read Matthew 25:14-30

In the Parable of the Talents, found in Matthew 25:14-30, Jesus teaches profound lessons on how to profit—not just in material wealth, but in spiritual and kingdom terms. The parable illustrates the responsibility of managing the resources God has entrusted to us, and the rewards for those who use them wisely.

The Parable Summary

A wealthy master, before going on a journey, entrusts his servants with different amounts of money, referred to as "talents" (a large sum of money). He gives five talents to one servant, two to another, and one to the third, according to their abilities. Upon his return, the master asks for an accounting. The servants who invested their talents wisely and made a profit are praised and rewarded with greater responsibility. However, the servant who hid his talent in fear and did nothing with it is reprimanded and cast away.

Key Teachings on How to Profit

God Entrusts Us with Resources

The master in the parable represents God, and the talents represent the resources, gifts, opportunities, and abilities He gives to each of us. Whether these talents are financial, intellectual, relational, or spiritual, they are all God's provision, entrusted to us for growth and increase. Jesus teaches that we must recognize that everything we have is a gift, and we are stewards of what God has provided.

Profiting Requires Action

Jesus emphasizes that profiting, or increasing what God has given, requires proactive effort. The two servants who were entrusted with five and two talents immediately put them to work, investing and trading to generate more. In contrast, the servant who received one talent was paralyzed by fear and chose to hide it instead of using it. Jesus is teaching that faithfulness and action are necessary for increase. Without taking risks or stepping out in faith, there can be no profit.

Stewardship Equals Responsibility

The parable illustrates that God expects us to manage what He gives us with responsibility. The servants were entrusted according to their abilities, which shows that God is fair in His expectations. We are not expected to use resources beyond our capacity, but we are accountable for how we handle what we've been given. The master's response to the profitable servants—"Well done, good and faithful servant" —shows that God rewards faithful stewardship.

Fear is the Enemy of Profit

The third servant's downfall was his fear. Instead of taking action, he buried his talent, afraid of losing it. Jesus teaches that fear of failure or the unknown can paralyze us and prevent us from stepping into the opportunities God has provided. In God's kingdom, fear is not an excuse for inaction. We are called to trust Him and take bold steps of faith, knowing that He will empower us.

Multiplying Talent is a Sign of Faithfulness

The servants who invested their talents and multiplied them demonstrated their faithfulness to the master. Jesus connects profit and increase with spiritual faithfulness. It's not just about making money or gaining more resources; it's about showing that we can be trusted with the little things so that God can entrust us with more. The act of multiplying, of making something grow, reflects a heart of trust and obedience to God.

Kingdom Profit is about More than Material Gain

While the parable involves financial talent, the deeper meaning goes beyond money. Profiting in the kingdom of God also involves growing in spiritual gifts, wisdom, and influence. It means investing our time, talents, and abilities for the advancement of God's kingdom—serving others, spreading the gospel, and using the unique gifts He has given us to bless the world. Kingdom profit is about eternal impact, not just earthly wealth.

Practical Application of How to Profit

To profit in the kingdom of God, we must first recognize that everything we have—whether time, money, skills, or relationships—is a resource given to us by God. We should:

- Invest in our skills and knowledge to multiply our ability to serve others and grow in wisdom.
- Step out in faith, taking risks where God leads, even when it feels uncomfortable or uncertain.
- Be faithful in small things, understanding that stewardship starts with what is in our hands right now.
- Live with purpose, using our resources to serve others and further God's kingdom, whether through business, ministry, or personal relationships.

The Reward for Profit

Jesus concludes the parable by showing that the faithful servants are rewarded with more responsibility and joy and entrusted with even greater opportunities. In the same way, when we steward what God gives us wisely, He promises to entrust us with more—both in this life and the life to come.

In the end, the parable teaches that true profit is not just about gaining more wealth, but about increasing the value of what God has given us, bringing honor to Him, and expanding His kingdom.

The Eternal Investment

In the FivestarMan message of authentic manhood, we teach five purposes God has deposited within men. Two of the purposes, the Entrepreneurial Drive and the Philanthropic Cause, seem to compete, yet they are complementary.

The Entrepreneurial Drive empowers you to gain wealth so that you are equipped to fulfill your purpose in life with the Philanthropic Cause.

One hand gathers, while the other hand scatters.

In the fleeting nature of life on earth, it is easy to become consumed by the pursuit of temporary wealth, comforts, and pleasures. Yet, as followers of Christ, we are called to a higher purpose—one that transcends the material and embraces the eternal.

This chapter explores the idea of Eternal Investment and the profound implications of tithing as an act of stewardship that aligns us with God's eternal economy.

Living and Leaving a Legacy

The concept of eternal investment is rooted in the understanding that everything we do today has lasting implications—both for our own lives and for those who come after us.

Our choices, the resources we manage, and the legacy we leave behind can echo throughout eternity.
Jesus spoke of storing up treasures in heaven, not on earth, where they are subject to decay and theft.

Matthew 6:19-21
"Do not store up for yourselves treasures on earth, where moths and vermin destroy, and where thieves break in and steal. But store up for yourselves treasures in heaven, where moths and vermin do not destroy, and where thieves do not break in and steal. For where your treasure is, there your heart will be also."

In this light, Tithing is an investment in eternity. When we worship God, we are sowing into the eternal realm rather than accumulating wealth for ourselves that will ultimately fade away.

Tithing, as a deliberate and faithful act of worship, becomes a way to deposit treasures in heaven, where they cannot be corrupted or lost.

Storing Up Treasures in Heaven

In Matthew 6:19-21, Jesus teaches His disciples not to lay up treasures on earth, where material possessions are vulnerable to decay, moths, rust, and thieves.

Instead, He urges us to store up treasures in heaven, a place where eternal value is measured differently—based not on material wealth but on the faithfulness of our hearts and actions. Every tithe we give, every act of generosity, is a deposit into an eternal account, one that will bring dividends not only for us but also for others in the kingdom of God.

The eternal nature of Tithing emphasizes that our giving is not simply a short-term transaction but a long-term investment. The blessings and rewards that God promises to those who give faithfully are far beyond what we can experience in this lifetime. When we choose to invest in the kingdom of God by returning a portion of what He has entrusted to us, we are participating in an eternal work that carries far-reaching consequences.

Investing in the Unseen Realm

While earthly investments are visible and tangible, eternal investments are often unseen and unmeasurable by worldly standards.

2 Corinthians 4:18

"So we fix our eyes not on what is seen, but on what is unseen. For what is seen is temporary, but what is unseen is eternal."

The eternal rewards for faithfulness in Tithing are not always immediately apparent. Yet, they are promised by God, who sees what is done in secret and rewards it openly (Matthew 6:4). Just as a farmer sows seeds with the hope of a harvest, so too do we sow our tithes in faith, trusting that God will bring an eternal harvest— one that will affect generations, bring souls to Christ, and multiply His kingdom.

Contrasting Temporary Wealth with True Riches

Jesus taught that the spirit of money — "mammon"—can become a stumbling block when we allow it to take precedence over God's will.
In Luke 16:11, Jesus says, *"So if you have not been trustworthy in handling worldly wealth, who will trust you with true riches?"*

Here, Jesus contrasts earthly wealth (mammon) with true riches—the eternal treasures that come from living in obedience to God's commands and using our resources for His kingdom.

Mammon represents this world's fleeting, temporary wealth that can be spent, lost, or stolen.

True riches, however, are eternal. They are the souls we touch, the good works we do in His name, and the spiritual rewards we will receive when we meet our Savior face to face. Tithing and investing in the kingdom of God reveals our trust in Him as the ultimate source of provision, and it aligns our hearts with the eternal purposes of His kingdom.

When we give our tithes faithfully, we demonstrate that our hearts are not bound by the fleeting desires of the world but are anchored in the eternal promise of God's kingdom. We are entrusted with true riches when we handle the temporary (mammon) with the understanding that it is a tool for fulfilling God's purposes, rather than a treasure to be hoarded or worshiped.

The Legacy We Leave

Living with an eternal perspective transforms not only how we view our finances but also how we live our lives. Every decision we make, including our financial choices, can be an opportunity to leave a legacy that glorifies God. When we live in alignment with God's eternal purposes, we leave behind more than just material wealth—we leave a spiritual legacy.

The way we steward our resources, particularly through Tithing, shapes the legacy we pass on. This legacy is not limited to what we leave our children or loved ones in terms of finances, but it extends to the values, faith, and practices we impart to the next generation. A legacy of faithful giving teaches others to prioritize the eternal over the temporal, investing in God's kingdom with a focus on His purposes rather than their own.

In Matthew 25:21, Jesus commends the faithful servant: *"Well done, good and faithful servant; you have been faithful with a few things; I will put you in charge of many things. Come and share your master's happiness."*

This passage speaks not only of personal reward but of a broader kingdom impact. By living in obedience and investing in God's eternal purposes through tithing, we set the stage for future generations to do the same, multiplying the blessings of God for years to come.

Practical Steps to Invest in Eternity

1. Make Tithing a Priority
Start by faithfully returning the first portion of your income to God, understanding that it is an act of worship and an investment in His kingdom.

2. Focus on Eternal Purposes
Shift your mindset from accumulating earthly wealth to seeking God's will in every area of your life. Ask God to help you align your priorities with His eternal plan.

3. Be Generous with Your Time and Talents
Beyond financial giving, invest your time and talents in serving others, advancing the gospel, and furthering the causes of God's kingdom on earth.

4. Teach Others to Give
Pass on the principles of faithful stewardship and eternal investment to the next generation, teaching them to live with an eternal perspective.

The Eternal Investment

Tithing is not just about giving money—it's about acknowledging God's sovereignty over all that we have and choosing to invest in something that will outlast us: the eternal kingdom of God.

In a world obsessed with temporary gain, Jesus calls us to focus on eternal investments that bring glory to God and bear fruit that lasts forever. As we live in obedience, store up treasures in heaven, and handle mammon faithfully, we are entrusted with true riches—the reward of eternal life and the fulfillment of God's purposes on earth.

A Legacy to Live For

As a man, you carry within you the power to shape the future—not only for yourself but for generations to come.

The choices you make today ripple out, touching the lives of those around you and those who will follow. You are not just living for the present moment, but for a purpose that extends beyond your lifetime.

Every decision you make, every action you take, is an opportunity to build a legacy that speaks of your values, your faith, and your commitment to something greater than yourself.

You are uniquely designed, with gifts, talents, and experiences that no one else has. The world needs your contribution. The people around you need your leadership, your wisdom, and your courage.

Whether in your family, your community, or your work, you are a vital link in the chain of a greater story—one that God has been weaving long before you arrived and will continue long after you're gone.

Living with intention means understanding that life is not a fleeting moment. It's an investment in the future.

What will you leave behind?

Will it be a legacy of integrity, of love, of sacrifice, of faithfulness?

Will it be a legacy that inspires others to dream, to give, to serve, and to build?

Your choices matter. Your actions today are shaping the world tomorrow.

Live boldly, knowing that you are creating a lasting impact. Pursue the things that matter most, invest in what is eternal, and be the man who leaves a legacy worth following. You are not just living for yourself—you are living for a future you will never see, but one that will remember you for the way you honored God and loved others.

Make it count. Live your life in a way that echoes into eternity. You were made for more than just the here and now—you were made to leave a legacy.